EVELYNE DE LA CHENELIÈRE

Evelyne de la Chenelière lives and works in Montréal. She trained at Michel Granvale à Paris and with Pol Pelletier, and works as both an actress and a writer. Her work for the theatre includes *Désordre public* (FTA/Théâtre Pàp); *Bashir Lazhar* (La Compagnie); *L'héritage de Darwin* (Théâtre Le Clou); *Chinoiserie* (À Tour de rôle); *Les hommes aiment-ils le sexe, vraiment autant qu'ils le disent?* (Espace Go); *Aphrodite en 04, La voix des autres, Henri & Margaux, Nicht retour, Mademoiselle* (Nouveau Théâtre Expérimental); *Culpa* (Productions Méa). Awards include a La Soirée des Masque for *Les Fraises en Janvier* in 2000, and the Governer General's Award for her collection *Désordre public*.

RONA MUNRO

Rona was born in Aberdeen a
film, radio and television. The
commissioned by the Edinbur̩ .... (Royal
Lyceum, Edinburgh); *The House of Bernarda Alba* (National Theatre of Scotland); *The Dirt Under the Carpet* (Paines Plough and Òran Mór); *Long Time Dead* (Paines Plough and Plymouth Theatre Royal); *Strawberries in January* (Traverse Theatre, Edinburgh); *Watership Down* (stage adaptation for the Lyric Theatre, Hammersmith); *Mary Barton* (Royal Exchange, Manchester); *The Indian Boy* (Royal Shakespeare Company); *Iron* (Traverse Theatre, winner of the John Whiting Award); *The Maiden Stone* (Hampstead Theatre and Royal Lyceum Theatre, Edinburgh; Peggy Ramsay Memorial Award Winner); *Gilt* (co-writer); *Bold Girls* (Susan Smith Blackburn Award, Evening Standard Most Promising Playwright Award, Plays International Award, Critics' Circle and Plays and Players Most Promising Playwright Award). Rona has written over twenty-five shows for the touring theatre company The MsFits. Film credits include *Ladybird Ladybird* directed by Ken Loach (FilmFour/Parallax Pictures Ltd); *Aimee and Jaguar* (Senator Film Production). For television, recent credits include: *Rehab* (BBC2); *Almost Adult* (Channel 4). Rona wrote five of the plays in the Stanley Baxter Playhouse series for Catherine Bailey Ltd/BBC Radio 4.

Other Titles in this Series

STRAWBERRIES IN JANUARY

by
Evelyne de la Chenelière

In a version by Rona Munro

From an original translation by Christopher Campbell

NICK HERN BOOKS

London
www.nickhernbooks.co.uk

A Nick Hern Book

Strawberries in January first published in 2006 by Nick Hern Books Limited, 14 Larden Road, London W3 7ST in association with the Traverse Theatre, Edinburgh

Cover image: Anna Crolla, featuring Gabriel Quigley as Sophie

Typeset by Country Setting, Kingsdown, Kent, CT14 8ES
Printed and bound in Great Britain by CLE Print Ltd, St Ives, Cambs, PE27 3LE

A CIP catalogue record for this book is available from the British Library

ISBN   978 1 85459 954 4

Strawberries in January was first performed at the Traverse
Theatre, Edinburgh, on 1 August 2006 with the following cast:

FRANCOIS   Paul Thomas Hickey
ROBERT   Phil McKee
SOPHIE   Gabriel Quigley
LEA   Lesley Hart

Director   Roxana Silbert
Designer   Emma Williams
Lighting Designer   Chahine Yavroyan
Sound Designer   Colin Pink

Characters

ROBERT

FRANCOIS

SOPHIE

LEA

Scene One

A spring morning, FRANCOIS*'s café.*

FRANCOIS *is drinking coffee and writing on his laptop. The sound of the bell on the café door.* ROBERT *enters.*

ROBERT. Hi, I don't know if you remember me?

FRANCOIS. Robert.

ROBERT. You eh . . . well you told me that you worked here so I just thought I'd drop in for a coffee before I went to teach my class . . .

FRANCOIS. Yeah that's great. How are you?

ROBERT. Oh you know, the usual, working too hard, how about you?

FRANCOIS. Fine thanks. I like mornings, when there's no one here, I get some peace to write.

ROBERT. Oh I won't stay long I . . .

FRANCOIS (*interrupts*). No, no, it's good to see you . . . go on . . . have a seat . . . really. So, did you finish that marking when you got back the other night?

ROBERT. Oh that, yes, I think I might have been quite generous for once. Drink, you know? My students are in for a surprise there. I couldn't concentrate. I kept thinking about that story you told me . . .

FRANCOIS. Oh that. Drink, you know? I don't usually talk about that. Especially not to someone I've barely met. I hope I didn't ramble on . . .

ROBERT. No, no, not at all, that's partly why I came, to hear the end of your story.

FRANCOIS. You want to hear about that *now*? (*Going to make coffee.*) What do you take in your coffee?

ROBERT. Nothing thanks. Now when you described that whole scene, the young woman, the suitcase . . . as something Sophie staged, to see if you really loved her . . . ?

3

FRANCOIS. Oh I don't know, I was probably just havering, mind you she did have a way of organising things, that girl . . . She'd this trick of arranging everything to suit her own ideas and then convincing you that it had been your idea all along. You know what I mean? One time, she came in here, and she was glowing. She'd picked her day you see? The sort of light that'd make a garden slug look like a wee bit of heaven. Imagine this woman, a woman who's radiant anyway, bathed in a golden glow . . .

ROBERT. Eh . . . OK.

SOPHIE *enters in her heavy winter coat.*

SOPHIE. Hullo François.

FRANCOIS. Hi, this is a nice surprise.

SOPHIE. It gets better.

She offers him a punnet of strawberries.

FRANCOIS. She offered me a basket of blushing strawberries, so red they made *me* blush. And they weren't in season . . . this was the middle of winter.

SOPHIE. I stopped by the market.

FRANCOIS. Thanks. That's nice of you. Do you want a . . . ?

SOPHIE (*cutting in*). Decaf. I've already had one.

FRANCOIS. Aren't you working today?

SOPHIE. Yes, but I'm going to be late because I have something to say to you.

FRANCOIS. What's wrong?

SOPHIE. I know this isn't the way you're supposed to do it and that is a bit of a worry but I said to myself life's short and if everyone always waits for everyone else to make the first move you can waste an awful lot of time and I know you sometimes watch me sleeping I know because I'm not actually sleeping and you can't deny it, yesterday for instance you were watching me sleeping and I know when we're drinking wine and talking in the sitting room together until two in the morning it's just agony for both of us to go to our separate beds and even if every couple tears each other apart and we've both made fun of all those couples that tear each other apart I think we owe it to ourselves to try and grab something that might tear us apart. And I don't see why if we like shopping together, doing the housework together, eating breakfast together, watching old films together, I don't really see why we wouldn't like making love together, because that's something a lot more exciting, it seems to me, than shopping, housework, and old films so I'm asking you to marry me in the spring. I know, conventionally I'm not supposed to be the one who asks but you prefer the unconventional so I'm asking you to marry me in the spring. Or outside, next winter, because it's conventional to get married in spring.

ROBERT. She just came out with it like that?

FRANCOIS. Yeah.

ROBERT. So what did you say?

FRANCOIS. I didn't say anything.

SOPHIE. You're not saying anything?

FRANCOIS. I knew it was the moment when I would have kissed her or something . . .

SOPHIE. That was the moment when you would have kissed me or something so I don't really know what to say now.

ROBERT. Why didn't you kiss her!?

FRANCOIS. But I couldn't even begin to feel worthy of this gift she was offering me, no embarrassment, no false modesty just . . . (*To* SOPHIE.) I'm just a bit surprised.

SOPHIE. I tried this out, in front of the mirror this morning to see how it came over and I thought I was quite moving?

ROBERT. Yes. It's very moving.

FRANCOIS. Yes. It's very moving.

SOPHIE. I suppose we can talk about it tonight.

ROBERT. And she left?

FRANCOIS. Yes, and you know what she did that made me want to marry her?

ROBERT. What?

FRANCOIS. When she was leaving she pushed the door instead of pulling.

SOPHIE *can't get out the door.*

ROBERT. What?

SOPHIE *is struggling with the door.*

5

FRANCOIS. Obviously she wanted to leave as fast as possible, well of course she did. I was struck dumb. That must have been unbearable for her. But she couldn't actually manage a dignified exit through the door, even though she was completely familiar with the door, even though we'd been flatmates for two years and I'd always worked in this café and she'd often visited me in this café and it had always been the same door – you have to push the door to get in and pull it to leave. She made such a sweet mess of it, fighting with the door, pushing it instead of pulling it, that it really touched me. I said to myself I'll never get bored with a woman who pushes doors instead of pulling them.

SOPHIE *finally succeeds in leaving.*

ROBERT. You said that?

FRANCOIS (*to himself*). I'll never get bored with a woman who pushes doors instead of pulling them. (*To* ROBERT.) Yes. I said that.

ROBERT. And then what?

FRANCOIS. Ach well, we never got married, you know that . . . Here I'm talking too much again, don't you have to teach a class?

ROBERT. Oh shit, my class. OK. I better go. What do I owe you?

ROBERT *rummages in his pockets.*

FRANCOIS. No, no you're alright . . . So drop in again yeah?

ROBERT. That'd be good, thanks. I'll see you then.

FRANCOIS (*to the audience*). He watched Robert walking away and he thought to himself that he'd found not only an amazing listener but the model for a true romantic hero. And he also thought that going dancing with Sophie that night was probably going to be really bad for his mental health.

Scene Two

Evening the same day, FRANCOIS *and* SOPHIE *are slow-dancing in a bar.*

SOPHIE. François?

FRANCOIS. What?

SOPHIE. Isn't it good we can still dance together?

FRANCOIS. Oh yeah.

6

SOPHIE. Even when we're totally decrepit it'll still be good to go dancing together. Alright?

FRANCOIS. Alright. But what about when your husband smashes my face in?

SOPHIE. What husband?

FRANCOIS. Come on Sophie. It'll happen. You know it will.

SOPHIE. Yeah, yeah.

FRANCOIS. He may be in this bar right now, shrivelling up with jealousy as he watches us and he's saying to himself, 'What is such an incomparable young woman doing in the arms of such a deeply ordinary human being?'

ROBERT *enters.*

SOPHIE. OK. Knock it off.

ROBERT. What is such an incomparable young woman doing in the arms of such a deeply ordinary human being?

FRANCOIS. And then he'd say, 'Pardon me miss . . .'

ROBERT *steps in front of* SOPHIE.

ROBERT. . . . but I think your partner's trousers clash rather unpleasantly with your skirt. That's not a good match at all . . . Therefore I feel I have to draw your attention to the degree to which your skirt and my trousers could form a wonderfully harmonious aesthetic union.

SOPHIE *starts to laugh and begins dancing with* ROBERT.

FRANCOIS. And he'd make you really laugh. You know I think that's the hardest thing women ever ask men to do, to make them laugh. For their whole lives. Their whole lives. Think about that. Still it's like my mother used to say, 'If they're laughing you're laughing . . . ' Then he'd say –

ROBERT. You know everyone gets married with no idea what they're doing. Let's have no idea what we're doing. Let's get married and work it out later. Like everyone else.

FRANCOIS. And you'd say . . .

SOPHIE. What's your surname?

FRANCOIS. Sophie, that's just too pragmatic.

SOPHIE. Alright. I'd say, 'I'll accept on condition that we replace the wedding march with Mozart's coronation mass.'

FRANCOIS. There you go.

ROBERT *exits.*

SOPHIE. You always think everything's a film.

FRANCOIS. Everything's better in films.

SOPHIE. The music makes it better.

FRANCOIS. That's it.

Scene Three

Flashback. LEA*'s B&B.* LEA *is absorbed in her reading.*
ROBERT, *a guest, watches her for a moment before speaking.*

ROBERT. Excuse me miss . . . ?

LEA (*still reading*). Yes.

ROBERT. I didn't sleep very well. This is a lovely little place,
    really, but . . .

LEA. Thanks.

ROBERT. But . . . Alright, I don't want to embarrass you. I'm not
    saying anything about the cleanliness of your establishment
    but . . . I have to tell you . . . the thing is . . . I found a dead
    mouse at the end of my bed.

LEA. . . .

ROBERT. Eh . . . did you hear me?

LEA. I'm just finishing this bit . . .

ROBERT. Miss? There was a dead mouse. At the end of my bed.
    That is to say practically in my bed.

LEA. OK, yeah. It was dead. It wasn't making any noise. How did
    it stop you sleeping?

ROBERT. Well . . . I had sort of a panic attack and I . . . are you
    telling me this is normal . . . ?

LEA. . . .

ROBERT. It's normal?

LEA. I'm just finishing this bit.

ROBERT. Because I don't want to come over like one of those city
    types who can't appreciate the joys of the country. In fact my
    room doesn't even have a functioning television and I'm coping
    perfectly happily, I promise you . . . But . . . a dead mouse . . . ?

8

You don't seem very alarmed. This is a regular event? It isn't considered unusual in rural areas like this?

LEA. You sound as if you're making a documentary on native customs. Stop it.

ROBERT. No, I didn't mean . . . sorry, I didn't mean to offend you.

LEA. . . .

ROBERT. What are you reading?

LEA *shows him the book.*

Well, there's a funny thing. I'm reading exactly the same book.

LEA. I know, its your book. I borrowed it when I came to change the sheets.

ROBERT. . . .

LEA. Is that a problem?

ROBERT. No, no. It's just . . .

LEA. I'm nearly finished. I'll bring it back.

ROBERT. Thanks. And . . . about the mice?

LEA. Don't worry about it. My cat must like you.

ROBERT. I see . . . it was . . . a sort of present was it?

LEA. That's it. A welcome gift. Flowers from me, mice from him. Don't let him upset you.

ROBERT. Oh right . . . thanks for the flowers. They've a wonderful smell haven't they . . . flowers.

LEA. You've underlined some odd passages. Why do you write in your books?

ROBERT. Because I'm a professor of literature and . . .

LEA. Oh, you teach.

ROBERT. Well, I'm sort of on a year's sabbatical of indefinite duration . . . but I still prepare exams, essay topics, I'm keeping my hand in. I'm glad you like the book.

LEA. Yeah, this guy's really good.

ROBERT. Eh . . . It was a woman.

LEA. Oh come on, his name's George.

ROBERT. Ah, but George Sand was the pseudonym of a romantic novelist who wrote under the name because . . .

LEA *is laughing.*

What?

LEA. I'm winding you up. I know who George Sand is. I just wanted to watch you playing Professor.

ROBERT. Oh right. Sorry. I should have realised.

LEA. Shouldn't you though.

ROBERT. OK good. I'm going to take a little walk. Is there a particular trail you'd recommend?

LEA. I'm not working tomorrow. If you like I can show you all that tomorrow.

ROBERT. Good, yes. That'd be nice.

LEA. OK, I'm going up. You know they said it would rain?

ROBERT. Oh yes, I know, I just want to stretch my legs a little.

LEA. You're not annoyed. That's very nice of you. Some of the guests get very annoyed with me when it rains, anyone would think they'd paid for sunshine as well as bed and breakfast.

ROBERT. Rain is good. Afterwards the grass has that wonderful smell of wet grass.

Scene Four

FRANCOIS*'s café.*

FRANCOIS. Earth to Robert?

ROBERT. Oh, I was thinking about a woman, as usual.

FRANCOIS. We wouldn't have much to talk about without them would we?

ROBERT. No.

FRANCOIS. What I say is, never a flatmate.

ROBERT. Never what?

FRANCOIS. Never fall in love with your flatmate.

ROBERT. Why?

FRANCOIS. Because she already knows too much! She knows that I snore, that I'm scared of mice, that I call my mother every day . . . You can't build a relationship out of that. It's impossible.

ROBERT. I always give fair warning, no commitment, no long-term plans, no domestic routines, no tears. There's only room for one toothbrush in my bathroom and that's mine. Don't expect me to give you family life, kids, Christmas puddings, any of the traditional stuff.

FRANCOIS. You tell them that?

ROBERT. Every time. The annoying thing is they always think they'll be the exception to the rule.

FRANCOIS. All of them?

ROBERT. Apart from the exceptions. The exceptions never realise they are exceptions.

FRANCOIS. God I'd love to understand women. Wouldn't you love that?

ROBERT. It might turn out to be a disappointment.

FRANCOIS. It might.

ROBERT. I'll tell you what I don't understand. Do you really never see Sophie? You've no idea what's happened to her? Your paths never cross?

FRANCOIS. No. I just hope she's found a better man than me.

ROBERT. What about the girl with the suitcase?

FRANCOIS. Never saw her again. I don't know if I'd recognise her in the street without a suitcase.

ROBERT. You left Sophie for a woman you wouldn't recognise on the street without a suitcase?

FRANCOIS. I didn't cancel the wedding because of her. It was because of her story.

ROBERT. I don't understand.

FRANCOIS. She came here, we weren't open yet.

LEA *enters, she's about eight months pregnant.*

We're closed!

LEA. You could have locked the door if you were closed.

FRANCOIS. There's a sign on the door. 'Closed.'

LEA. When do you open?

FRANCOIS. When it suits me. My place, my rules.

LEA. And here's me saying to myself, 'At last, something's open in this dirty town with its never ending winter,' and now you're telling me you're shut. I'm not going without a cup of something. I'm sorry, but I arrived at the bus station and I just can't drink anything in those twenty-four-hour places, I think it's the fluorescent lights, I'll have a decaf please, just to get off my feet. You see you seem nice. Even when you said 'We're closed!' in that gruff unfriendly voice I could tell you were nice, otherwise I'd've been out the door right away. I'm a bit on edge at the minute. I hate cities. I came here to find my friend. Though actually I don't know her, I don't know her any more, we were friends when we were ten, her family moved house and we lost touch, she's the only real friend I've ever had. Nothing's ever mattered as much since apart from this one man . . .

ROBERT. I don't understand.

FRANCOIS. I don't understand what you mean.

LEA. I think we fell in love.

ROBERT. 'We' who?

FRANCOIS. 'We' who?

LEA. He was a man of mystery, like in the films. A tourist, a restless traveller, very beautiful, a little bit sad but not too much. I knew he'd be moving on in a few days. We still made a baby. Outside. A baby who'll have that wonderful smell of wet grass.

ROBERT. Wet grass?

LEA. I have to find my girlfriend. We used to write to each other now and then. I was walking round and round looking for her then I realised I was looking for a ten-year-old girl. Daft. I know perfectly well she isn't ten years old anymore. She's got a two-year-old daughter. She wrote to me about her last year, I didn't answer. I could search the streets for a two-year-old girl who looks like my ten-year-old friend. In her letter she said she'd be moving into a new house soon. But I don't have her new address. She stopped writing to me. I hope she isn't dead.

ROBERT. Her baby, was it a boy or a girl?

FRANCOIS. What? I didn't ask. (*To* LEA.) What's your friend's name?

LEA. Sophie.

ROBERT. Sophie?

LEA. I'll find her.

ROBERT. What about the baby's father?

FRANCOIS. What about the baby's father? Aren't you looking for him?

LEA. He was a tourist, a restless traveller, an explorer trying to find his freedom. I have to see my friend. Look . . . I don't like hotels and I'm sure my friend will look after me when I find her . . . can I stay with you just till then?

FRANCOIS. . . .

ROBERT. And?

LEA. You seem a bit taken aback.

FRANCOIS. It's just I'm living with this woman and . . .

LEA. Do you love her?

FRANCOIS. We're getting married next week.

LEA. No, I'm sorry, it's quite alright, I understand. I just want to wash my hair. I left in a hurry and then there was the endless bus journey, eight hours, I'd love to wash my hair, I wouldn't make a mess. But I've frightened you, I'm so sorry, I do understand, I've probably forgotten how to behave myself in the big city. Be happy with this woman, don't ever be nervous, be wonderful. I'm much better now. I'll look for my friend and then I can wash my hair.

FRANCOIS. Wait! Are you going to be alright?

LEA. Thank you. Of course I will.

FRANCOIS. What are you going to do?

LEA. I'm going to find my friend.

ROBERT. And did she find her friend?

FRANCOIS. Wait!

LEA. What?

FRANCOIS *is writing his telephone number on a book of matches.*

FRANCOIS. Do me a favour. Call me and let me know if you've found your friend.

ROBERT. And she never called?

LEA. So your wife can pick up and chew my ear off?

13

She looks at the book of matches FRANCOIS *is holding out.*

Is that your real phone number?

ROBERT. Why did she say that?

LEA. Because someone once told me that when a man writes his number on a book of matches it's usually a fake.

FRANCOIS. That's my telephone number.

LEA. François, that's a nice name.

ROBERT. And her name? What was her name?

FRANCOIS. But your name? What's your name? Wait . . . !

LEA *doesn't hear. She's already left.*

She never called me.

ROBERT. You don't know where she came from? What she did?

FRANCOIS. No, I never had a chance to ask.

ROBERT. That's extraordinary . . . She was probably mad, overwrought anyway. Still, you're right, sometimes the strangest things can be seductive. I had a student who got under my skin like that, with a story . . . I had no idea at first . . . she handed in one essay, then another, all on very different subjects, required subjects, until one day I realised I was desperate to read her essays. Really desperate. And I wouldn't sit in my office to read them like I did with the others, I'd get into bed so I could read her words just before I fell asleep. You see if you put her essays back to back they made a continuous narrative, a story. She wrote her first novel like that. By completing her essay assignments.

FRANCOIS. And you fell in love with her?

ROBERT. Well unfortunately she wasn't what you'd call good-looking.

FRANCOIS. Ah.

ROBERT. But a literary genius.

FRANCOIS. But not good-looking?

ROBERT. No.

FRANCOIS. So you like good-looking women yeah?

ROBERT. Do you know a man who doesn't like good-looking women?

FRANCOIS. There are women like that aren't there, where it just seems so unfair that they're not good-looking.

ROBERT. Yeah. And then there's the good-looking women who ought to be ugly.

LEA. . . . Hey maybe you could set me essay titles so I could finally write something with a bit of structure or . . .

ROBERT. You wouldn't want to do that, surely.

FRANCOIS. What's the subject you're setting your students at the moment?

ROBERT. Well actually talking of my students, I better get going if I don't want to stand them up. (*Looking for money.*)

FRANCOIS. No don't worry about the coffee . . .

ROBERT. Thanks very much, so I'll . . .

FRANCOIS. What's the topic? Just for a laugh.

ROBERT. 'The contemporary critic Georges Blanc wrote, in *Stendhal and the Problem of the Novel,* 'In spite of his having theoretically aligned himself with a programme of realistic tendencies, Stendhal fortunately never exposed the works of his imagination to its dangerous influence'. Discuss.

FRANCOIS. No, you're alright.

ROBERT. I'll come back tomorrow for the next instalment.

Scene Five

FRANCOIS*'s café.* ROBERT *watches* SOPHIE *and* FRANCOIS.

SOPHIE. How do you mean, 'you don't think you're ready'? You're joking aren't you?

FRANCOIS. It's just happening so fast . . .

SOPHIE. François, everything's fine. We're in love. We're planning a wedding here not an execution.

FRANCOIS. I know . . .

SOPHIE. It'll just be a brilliant party.

FRANCOIS. And then a life-long commitment.

SOPHIE. Look François, it's perfectly understandable you've got last-minute nerves.

FRANCOIS. I'm telling you. We've got to cancel Sophie. I'm sorry.

SOPHIE. You're sorry.

FRANCOIS. This is hurting me too.

SOPHIE. Oh I'm not hurt, I'm *raging.* Tell me the truth here François. Because a story about some pregnant woman washing up here with her suitcase might be great for the movie but I'm not buying it.

ROBERT. She didn't believe you?

FRANCOIS. You don't believe me?

SOPHIE. No. I don't believe you.

ROBERT. I don't blame her.

FRANCOIS. I don't blame you.

SOPHIE. Have you been playing around? Is that it?

FRANCOIS. God no!

SOPHIE. You've been led astray by some girl buying a cup of coffee and you don't know how to tell me?

FRANCOIS. No! This girl didn't lead me astray. She made me look the horrible truth in the face. And it made me dizzy because I realised I might do that, I might make a run for it one day. I might be completely freaked out at the idea of spending the rest of my days with a woman, I mean with only one woman. And I can't bear to imagine it, you, alone, pregnant, with a suitcase, all because, one day I've panicked.

ROBERT. Then what?

FRANCOIS. Well then it was really her pride that was talking.

SOPHIE. Oh you're the big man François. No really, far too big for me. Alright, you cancel the wedding. I don't want to hear anything more about it. You can tell everyone the story of the woman and the suitcase. That'll give them a good laugh. Cheers.

ROBERT. So was that it?

SOPHIE *tries to leave, she's having problems with the door of the café, pushing instead of pulling.*

FRANCOIS (*to* SOPHIE). That's it? (*To* ROBERT.) How do you mean, 'was that it?'

SOPHIE. Bastard door!

SOPHIE *manages to get out.*

ROBERT. Well didn't you run after her in the rain?

FRANCOIS. How do you mean, 'in the rain'?

ROBERT. I don't know – in the rain – just seems better.

FRANCOIS. In a film yeah, but in real life your trainers are soaked and your toes are swimming about in that weird rain gravy . . .

ROBERT. Point taken . . . OK I'm late again. How much do I owe you?

FRANCOIS (*handing him a script*). No you're alright, I owe you one . . . my screenplay.

ROBERT. Oh thanks! I'll give that a read.

ROBERT *leaves as* FRANCOIS *turns to* SOPHIE.

FRANCOIS. How do you mean, 'you don't think you're ready'? You're joking aren't you?

SOPHIE. I'm not in love François. I thought I was but I was wrong. I really like you but . . .

FRANCOIS. You're going to tell me you just want to be friends.

SOPHIE. . . . Yes.

FRANCOIS. God you wouldn't believe the number of friends I've got. The whole world wants to be my friend. All the women I know want me to be their friend, their brother, their big cuddly teddy bear. Talk about lucky, I'm swimming in female friendship.

SOPHIE. No stop it François, tell me you don't hate me, tell me we can still be friends.

FRANCOIS. I've got dozens of wonderful friends. Why would I need your friendship?

SOPHIE. I know you're disappointed François . . .

FRANCOIS. Disappointed? I'm disappointed when I miss the previews at the cinema. Don't talk to me about disappointed.

SOPHIE. Bastard door!

FRANCOIS. You have to pull it Sophie. Pull it!

SOPHIE *manages to exit.*

He reflected that he should have told her to stay instead of telling her to pull the door. Or maybe run after her in the rain, though, unfortunately, there was gorgeous sunshine that day. He

thought again about the screenplay he'd just given Robert. At
once he regretted having given him the true version of the facts
to read.

Scene Six

LEA *addresses the audience.*

LEA. Dearest Sophie, how are you keeping? I'm doing pretty good.
I tried to find you in Montreal but I didn't have your new
address. I have a little boy now, François. He's two-and-a-half
months old. When he was born in January he looked like a big
red strawberry, a wee bit lost in the middle of all the white. He
resembles his father enough to ensure I can never forget the
restless traveller I told you about in my last letter. Which you
didn't get obviously. He was the kind of man who suits his age.
Who'll thrill all the young women who're sexually aroused by a
wee bit of grey at a man's temples.

How is your wee Lea? That really touched me you know, that
you called your daughter Lea. If I'd had a girl I would have
called her Sophie, I promise. It was a deal after all. I hope your
husband is still spoiling you rotten. I know you deserve it. He
sounds wonderful.

When I go into the village everyone gives me weird looks. A
single mum is a real oddity round here. If you were here you
could help me laugh at them all.

I've opened up the bed and breakfast for the summer. There was
this couple on their honeymoon. They're the worst, couples on
their honeymoon. They left early because François isn't going
through the night. OK François does have a penetrating voice.
But it was nothing compared to the racket of those two making
love and I told them so. I told them they weren't being very
sensitive to my feelings. If I ever change jobs it won't be
because of breakfasts at dawn or broken taps at two in the
morning, it'll be because of all the noise of folk making love
when I'm lying all alone in my bed. When the b and b is full I
feel like I'm running a bordello, I'm telling you.

Apart from that I'm well. I'm waiting for you to write to me and
give me your address so I can send this letter. I hope you and
your little family will visit me one day.

See you soon, Lea

Scene Seven

SOPHIE *and* FRANCOIS *are walking outside, eating a sandwich.*

FRANCOIS (*to audience*). He still saw Sophie nearly every day and she told him, in all innocence, about her latest conquests. Usually Italians. He said to himself he should really learn Italian one of these days.

SOPHIE. . . . an Italian. He'd been to the clinic a couple of times with his dog, a beautiful black Labrador with arthritis, and we sort of noticed each other. So anyway, he asked me out to dinner . . .

FRANCOIS. The Labrador?

SOPHIE. No! The Italian.

FRANCOIS. Right. I should really learn Italian one of these days.

SOPHIE. And we had a lovely evening. He's such a gentleman, so sophisticated. And you know me, talk to me in Italian and I'm a puddle on the floor.

FRANCOIS. Doesn't he speak French?

SOPHIE. Yeah, 'course, but at the end of the evening he told me he just couldn't stop himself slipping into Italian when he talked about love.

FRANCOIS. Aw that's so *sweet.*

SOPHIE. You just hate romance.

FRANCOIS. I just hate schmaltz.

SOPHIE. Well I'd like to see how you'd declare love to a woman.

FRANCOIS. I've already declared love to you.

SOPHIE. Right, and it wasn't romantic at all.

Lighting change, flashback, launderette.

FRANCOIS. How can you say I'm not romantic? You know your problem, you've had an overdose of Hollywood, you think there ought to be this beautiful, tear-jerking background music . . .

SOPHIE. It's just we're in a launderette, with horrible strip lighting and suddenly you tell me you know you're in love with me because you want to share a laundry basket? What do you want me to say to that?

FRANCOIS. Sophie, we've been flatmates for almost two years and I want to tell you that I know your little pots of cream and the bottles of perfume that invade the bathroom, I know your 'wee phone calls' that last three hours, I know that undrinkable, no-fat milk you're obsessed with buying, I know your Nutella emergencies at one in the morning, I know your menstrual cycle and the mood swings that go with it, I know how you look first thing in the morning with your hair all over the place, I know everything that could ever kill love between two people and it's made me fall in love with you. I think the underwear you try to hide when we're doing the laundry together is beautiful. I think your dirty washing is beautiful. I love standing outside your bedroom door in the evening listening to you breathe, waiting to hear the moment when you fall asleep, I love it when you lose it because I've put something recyclable in the dustbin, I love it when you take a sneaky look on my computer for the writing I don't want to show you . . .

SOPHIE. I hardly read a thing, I promise!

They kiss. Abrupt return to reality, eating sandwich.

FRANCOIS. Anyway . . . I hope it all goes well with your Italian.

SOPHIE. I mustn't get carried away but I have to admit I'm desperate to see him again. He was supposed to phone me last night . . .

FRANCOIS. Why didn't you call him?

SOPHIE. I've only got his mobile number, and that's sort of turned into a fax . . .

FRANCOIS. Eh?

SOPHIE. I don't know, it just made a weird noise . . . He'll definitely phone me today.

FRANCOIS. He gave you a fake number?

SOPHIE. No!

FRANCOIS. He gave you a fake number.

SOPHIE. You don't know him. He's not like that.

FRANCOIS. If you say so.

SOPHIE. François can you tell me why you have this idea that every guy I meet is a wanker?

FRANCOIS. That's not true.

SOPHIE. It is true. You're always telling me I'm wasting my time but do you ever make the effort to find me someone? No. You'll rubbish every man I meet but your friends are too good for me. Is that it?

FRANCOIS. I'm only trying to rescue you from this ridiculous vision of the ideal man that's polluted your wee brain! You think you're going to fall in love with some fucking cinematic cliche, you keep waiting for that, you keep waiting, you keep dreaming that it's just around the corner and now no one could ever be good enough for you!

SOPHIE. That's not true. That's rotten.

FRANCOIS. OK go ahead and sigh over your 'sophisticated' Italian, go ahead and suffer, looks like you enjoy it.

He exits.

Scene Eight

LEA. Hi Sophie.

I can't take the countryside any more. Way too much oxygen, too many trees, too much bird song. Beautiful scenery is doing my head in. I want dirty streets, car horns, smoky bars. Streets that look like they're boiling over with crazy ants, running in every direction at once, crashing and bashing into each other, never stopping.

I was really naive to think I could find you in Montreal without an address. I thought I could just go to a corner shop and say, 'Excuse me, where does Sophie Lamontagne live please?'. But that was never a good idea was it? How many corner shops must there be in Montreal?

I don't know where to send this letter, maybe I'll send it to every corner shop in Montreal . . .

Anyway I'll still write to you in the meantime. Give Lea a kiss and take a big breath of exhaust fumes for me.

Lea.

Scene Nine

FRANCOIS, *arms full of shopping, meets* ROBERT *ambling down the street.*

FRANCOIS. Robert! What are you doing here?

ROBERT. Oh, hullo François.

FRANCOIS. Aren't you working?

ROBERT. It's half term.

FRANCOIS. Right.

ROBERT. But they've still got reading to do, there's exams to prepare . . . I don't let them get bored.

FRANCOIS. So you haven't had time to read my screenplay then?

ROBERT. No, you see I had all this marking . . .

FRANCOIS. Brilliant.

ROBERT. I think the students are getting more stupid every year.

FRANCOIS. You know you always seem so relaxed but I bet you're tough on them.

ROBERT. They've no discipline, no courage, no determination. All they're interested in is getting away with doing as little as possible. It drives me crazy.

FRANCOIS. Do you like your job then?

ROBERT. Only because if I'm lucky, every few years there'll be one wee gem.

FRANCOIS. Like that ugly girl?

ROBERT. Yeah.

FRANCOIS. Yeah that haunts me, 'The ugly girl who writes like an angel,' because in the usual film scenario – the girl who writes like an angel and piques the curiosity of her literature professor – would be a total babe.

ROBERT. Otherwise the film wouldn't sell.

FRANCOIS. That's it.

ROBERT. . . .

FRANCOIS. Hey Robert?

ROBERT. What?

FRANCOIS. What are you doing next week? You must have bit more time over half term so I could have you round for dinner with a really good friend of mine. I'd love to introduce her to you.

ROBERT. That's a great idea. What's her name?

FRANCOIS. . . . Genevieve. She's called Genevieve.

ROBERT. That's pretty. What's she like?

FRANCOIS. Oh I think you'll like her, she's very easy-going, very uncomplicated, the sort of woman who knows what she wants.

ROBERT. Well call me, and I'll make sure I read your screenplay before that.

FRANCOIS. Oh no rush, you're alright . . . it's work in progress, I'll have a better version soon.

Scene Ten

FRANCOIS *is walking outside. He meets* SOPHIE.

FRANCOIS (*to audience*). As he walked towards his rendezvous with Sophie he thought of all the friends he'd hidden from her. Guys she might have liked. He began to list all Sophie's faults one by one, an exercise he performed from time to time which sometimes actually gave him peace of mind. Sophie is demanding, she's contradictory, she's often self-centred, she's a superficial thinker with middle-of-the-road attitudes. True. She bites her nails, not very ladylike. She asks too many questions and she's tactless. She's short-sighted, and when she blows her nose it is not a thing of beauty . . . (*Pause.*) When she bumps into a chair she says 'Sorry' to the chair. When she's nervous she does this really sweet thing where she fiddles with her hair and chews the end of it. When she laughs her eyes light up then they disappear into two wee dimples and . . . shit. François had miserably failed the exercise.

SOPHIE. No but lying? I won't have it. If he'd told me he was married, I might have taken a chance on being his lover – I might . . . but he wanted to hide it from me, I won't stand for that. I can't believe it, such a gorgeous Italian guy . . .

FRANCOIS. So sophisticated . . .

SOPHIE. Oh stop it.

FRANCOIS. Perhaps he just wanted to create a moment when he could *really* forget his wife, by staying faithful to you for one night. I think it's beautiful he didn't tell you the truth.

SOPHIE. François I don't quite see the point of that touching eulogy on lying so just spare me, OK?

FRANCOIS. The point is in the poetry, in the dream . . .

SOPHIE. François.

FRANCOIS. OK I am winding you up . . . look, the guy's a wanker. That's it.

SOPHIE. There you go.

FRANCOIS. . . .

SOPHIE. See what I want is really dead simple, just a stable relationship . . . my mother is so worried.

FRANCOIS. You're not doing this for your mother Sophie.

SOPHIE. No. But I can't bear it. Every time I go round for tea she lays an extra place 'in case I've found someone'. Then she tells me her story about meeting my Dad, again . . . She needles me . . . She nips at me. She says 'Of course you're only happy in casual relationships,' but it's not true! I want a family. I want kids. I want Christmas puddings, all the traditional stuff.

FRANCOIS. Sophie, I've got an idea. (*To audience.*) A really bad idea because, of course, he didn't actually want Sophie and Robert ever to meet. He wanted Sophie all to himself. Still, a meeting between Robert and Sophie was inevitable, otherwise the story would be too simple. And anyway there was nothing to be worried about because it was impossible Robert and Sophie would fall in love at first sight, unimaginable. He told himself he really had to stop being so jealous.

SOPHIE. So what's your idea?

FRANCOIS. I've got this friend, well, more of an acquaintance, he's just your type, a big good-looking guy, a bit like me, I met him at a book launch then he's dropped in at the café a few times. He's a professor of literature . . . he's very cultured . . . very sophisticated . . .

SOPHIE. Yeah? Why haven't you talked about him before?

FRANCOIS. I haven't known him long.

SOPHIE. You're sure he isn't married?

FRANCOIS. Actually he told me he's divorced.

SOPHIE. Right, so his ex-wife is still part of the furniture.

FRANCOIS. Not at all, they were only together two years, they didn't even have time to start a family.

SOPHIE. And physically?

FRANCOIS. Well, like I said, he's a big good-looking guy . . .

SOPHIE. No, her, his ex. What does she look like?

FRANCOIS. Why do you want to know that?

SOPHIE. If she's better looking than me I don't want to meet him.

FRANCOIS. You are so complicated! I've never seen his ex. I haven't known Robert that long.

SOPHIE. He's called Robert?

FRANCOIS. Well yeah . . .

SOPHIE. I'm not crazy about that.

FRANCOIS. Oh you're wearing me out Sophie!

SOPHIE. OK, OK, Robert. If he is a professor of literature that might work.

FRANCOIS. Great, I'll do dinner then. There's just one wee thing . . .

SOPHIE. What?

FRANCOIS. Now I don't want you to get cross . . .

SOPHIE. What is it?

FRANCOIS. You have to call yourself Genevieve.

SOPHIE. What!?

FRANCOIS. I told him your name was Genevieve.

SOPHIE. Why did you do that?

FRANCOIS. Well because . . . now this is for real OK? . . . because he's got a bit of a blockage about the name Sophie.

SOPHIE. Eh? How come?

FRANCOIS. His ex was called Sophie. I don't think it ended well.

SOPHIE. What kind of rubbish is that? Really.

FRANCOIS. No listen, it's just to smooth things along . . .

SOPHIE. My name is Sophie Lamontagne and that's it. He'll have to live with it.

FRANCOIS. Och details, details, Genevieve, Sophie – what does it matter if it keeps him happy?

SOPHIE. François, when we were flatmates I was prepared to lie on the phone to all sorts of women. I did that. For you. But this is a wee bit too much . . .

FRANCOIS. Come on Sophie, just to get us off to a good start, please, you'll see how great he is, you're going to be so good together. Pretend it's a game . . . he's really keen to meet you.

SOPHIE. You've told him about me?

FRANCOIS. A bit . . . .

SOPHIE. Did you tell him we used to go out together?

FRANCOIS. No no, no need for that eh?

SOPHIE. No, you're right.

FRANCOIS. Don't forget, 'Genevieve'.

SOPHIE. Alright . . . OK, but I think that's rubbish.

FRANCOIS. I'm sure he's the man for you. He's a bit older, the way you like them. I mean this is a mature man, responsible you know? And he's got a proper job, that'll please your mum.

SOPHIE. OK we better get a move on. Set it up for dinner tomorrow.

FRANCOIS. Jeez you don't waste any time do you?

SOPHIE. My child-bearing years are nearly over François.

FRANCOIS. You're twenty-eight!

SOPHIE. OK but by the time we've travelled a bit, moved in together, got past our crisis . . .

FRANCOIS. What d'you mean? Your crisis?

SOPHIE. Listen, you can't have kids without getting past at least one significant crisis, otherwise the relationship is doomed to failure. Didn't you know that?

FRANCOIS. Whatever. I'll give you a ring about dinner.

SOPHIE. Will you help me choose what to wear?

FRANCOIS. OK but I'm not doing four hours of it like that other time.

SOPHIE. I promise. Love you.

FRANCOIS. Cheerio then.

SOPHIE. François.

FRANCOIS. What?

SOPHIE. What are you going to tell him?

FRANCOIS. What?

26

SOPHIE. Robert, about me? What are you going to tell him?

FRANCOIS. How do I know . . . ?

SOPHIE. Don't give him the idea I'm really good-looking. He'll just get disappointed.

FRANCOIS. OK.

SOPHIE. Aye but tell him I'm quite good-looking, he needs to know another man thinks I'm good-looking.

FRANCOIS. OK, OK.

SOPHIE. Can you do my hair like I had it for my sister's wedding?

FRANCOIS. OK.

SOPHIE. Would that be too much?

FRANCOIS. Yes.

SOPHIE. Why did you say 'OK' if you think it'll look bogging?

FRANCOIS. I've got to get going Sophie, I'm late already.

SOPHIE. OK, I'll give you a ring.

FRANCOIS. Genevieve?

SOPHIE. Eh?

FRANCOIS. Just testing.

SOPHIE. Oh very droll.

Scene Eleven

LEA. Sophie, you never write and it's starting to annoy me. Don't try the 'busy mother' number with me. I'm a busy mother too. When I'm annoyed with François I'm so ashamed of myself. But he only annoys me as often as he makes me melt. I'd love to describe how cute he is how his innocence has reawakened my inner child and all the other stuff parents say but right now I'm just exhausted. I don't want him to turn round one day and say 'My mother was a nervous wreck, she went insane in her own bed and breakfast, toppled over the edge by too much fresh air and boredom. She sold everything she had for a song, claiming the B&B was haunted by the ghosts of all these couples howling in orgasm every night. She travelled the world to deliver letters for a Sophie Lamontagne to all the corner shops of Brazil, China, South America, every corner shop in the world . . . '

What I'd like to do would be to find my restless traveller again, and show him our baby and for that to be the best surprise anyone has ever given him.

I love him. Fear slipped in between us and took up all the space. So I didn't tell him. Maybe that was because of the joke he made too. Just before he left, he wrote me his telephone number on a book of matches.

ROBERT. Never trust a man who writes his telephone number on a book of matches. It's usually a fake number.

LEA. He didn't want it to be a heavy moment. Scared of looking ridiculous probably. So I didn't cry in front of him either. Is that what they mean by the unbearable lightness of being? When we played at grown-up ladies Sophie we never imagined any of this. We played happy, contented grown-up ladies, otherwise it wouldn't have been a proper game would it? Otherwise it would have been no fun at all. No little girl ever plays at single-parent ladies so maybe that's why I don't know how to do it very well, it's because I never got the practise. I love my baby so much. I watch him breathing, so regular and so peaceful and I just hope I'll be worthy of him all his life. But you'll know what I mean.

See you soon. Lea

Scene Twelve

Dinner at FRANCOIS*'s.* FRANCOIS *talks to the audience while* ROBERT *and* SOPHIE *are meeting each other.*

FRANCOIS. He bought everything from a caterer and transferred it onto his own plates. What the eye doesn't see . . . or whatever it is. He reminded himself you always see them eating a meal at some point in French films. The evening was off to a really good start.

SOPHIE. A professor of literature? Where?

ROBERT. At the University of Montreal.

SOPHIE. Oh hey me too, I was there, studying psychology.

ROBERT. Yes? Was this a long time ago?

SOPHIE. Not as long as all that.

ROBERT. Obviously not, excuse me.

SOPHIE. Hey maybe we've already bumped into each other in the corridors.

ROBERT. Right, yes. Maybe.

SOPHIE. Back then François and me were flatmates here, eh François?

FRANCOIS (*serving drinks*). Eh yeah . . . Robert, Genevieve, come and sit down for your aperitifs.

SOPHIE (*looking around*). There's been some stonking joints smoked in here . . . eh François?

FRANCOIS. Not that . . . stonking.

Awkward pause.

SOPHIE. Right! Let's have a toast!

FRANCOIS. To what?

SOPHIE. To our host.

FRANCOIS. To my friends.

Time passes. They are eating dessert.

ROBERT. It's not a question of establishing whether man is intrinsically good or bad but whether compassion is innate or the result of cultural influences.

SOPHIE. Well I think it's the little things people do that help the world, not all these big ideas.

ROBERT. Only considered thought and communication can stop us constantly making the same mistakes.

SOPHIE. Even if we're always talking the same crap?

FRANCOIS. Genevieve.

SOPHIE. What?

ROBERT. No, no, a bit of disagreement is good.

SOPHIE (*false innocence*). Oh I didn't specifically mean you. (*The pudding.*) This is lovely François.

ROBERT. It's excellent. I didn't know you could cook.

FRANCOIS *and* SOPHIE (*together*). Neither did I.

An awkward laugh.

ROBERT. You know people do have a tendency to defuse any debate for the sake of placid mediocrity.

SOPHIE. Oh that reminds me . . . (*To* ROBERT.) Sorry . . . (*To* FRANCOIS.) François, remember the philosophy teacher we had at college? He's only gone and married a student.

FRANCOIS. Yeah?

SOPHIE. Is that all you can say?

FRANCOIS. So what?

SOPHIE. So he was already forty-five when he was teaching us!

FRANCOIS. Well it's none of your business really is it Genevieve?

SOPHIE. I'm sure you wouldn't think of marrying one of your students at your age, would you Robert?

ROBERT. As it happens my ex-wife was initially a student of mine.

SOPHIE. And why not? You know what I say, as long as you've got love. The truth is everyone would rather think other people's lives were a disaster . . .

ROBERT. Yes we have great difficulty maintaining any proximity to another's happiness.

SOPHIE. So you're a pessimist?

ROBERT. No, don't mistake depth for darkness, no, I merely recognise that process of destruction which is particular to our species. Other animals manage things better than we do . . .

SOPHIE. I love animals.

FRANCOIS. Genevieve works in a veterinary clinic . . .

ROBERT. And I suppose that's why you're a vegetarian?

SOPHIE. Partly, but I like cats and dogs best and I never ate them anyway.

ROBERT. So basically you like everything you're supposed to like?

SOPHIE. What are you trying to say?

ROBERT. Well you like cats, dogs, you probably like children, Mozart, the countryside, supporting Aids charities . . .

SOPHIE. Why are you saying it like that? You think I'm ridiculous?

FRANCOIS. OK, who wants coffee?!

ROBERT. Not at all . . .

FRANCOIS. You know what we need? A wee digestif.

FRANCOIS *exits.*

ROBERT. . . . just that you're conventional. But don't worry, it's fashionable to be unconventional so you're original.

SOPHIE. And is your opinion of people always based on theories like that?

ROBERT. I'm logical, that's all.

SOPHIE. Some logic. Listen, what you need to understand is I don't like Mozart just because 'you're supposed to like Mozart'. I really love that guy, OK? You've no right to generalise about my genuine love for his music. If anyone today could come up with one bar of music worthy of Mozart, that man could die in peace. You've really annoyed me now!

ROBERT. I'm sorry Genevieve, I didn't mean to upset you.

SOPHIE. I'm not surprised you're François's friend. Peas in a pod . . .

ROBERT. Were you two together?

SOPHIE. . . . the same lack of humility. The same determination to wave your little ideas around as if they were *so* big . . .

ROBERT. Ah, you were together.

SOPHIE. How do you think you know that?

ROBERT. How long was this?

SOPHIE. Did he tell you?

ROBERT. A long time?

SOPHIE. When?

ROBERT. When what?

SOPHIE. When did he tell you?

ROBERT. About what?

SOPHIE. About us.

ROBERT. About us?

SOPHIE. What?

ROBERT. What?

SOPHIE. I'm asking you how you know that François and me were together?

ROBERT. Ah! I don't know . . . a kind of intimacy, something that never entirely disappears between two people who've ever said 'I love you.' Even though it's far easier for two people to hate each other once they've made love they'll still be linked forever because they share the same secret.

SOPHIE. You see? You've got this way of saying things as if you were the bearer of truth. It's irritating.

ROBERT. I just try to get a little distance on things. I'm very critical of people but I love them deeply. I love human beings because they always strive to be great, to be beautiful, to be happy. They can never achieve it but I find their vain attempts very moving.

SOPHIE. And there you go again, talking about being human as if you're not, as if you were making a documentary – 'A day in the life of a goldfish.' Why are you laughing?

ROBERT. I'm not making fun of you. I'm smiling because I actually like it when someone stands up to me.

SOPHIE. Oh right. Thanks.

ROBERT. My ex-wife had this way of agreeing with everything I said. That might explain why I've been left with a few pretentious tendencies.

SOPHIE. 'Sophie' wasn't it? You know that's a pretty name.

ROBERT. What?

SOPHIE. Your ex-wife was called Sophie wasn't she?

ROBERT. No. Why?

SOPHIE. No? Oh, OK, sorry, I must be getting confused.

ROBERT. Anyway, now you know all my faults I hope I'll get the chance to show you my good side . . .

SOPHIE. Didn't your ex-wife find out your faults?

FRANCOIS *re-enters.*

ROBERT. Not really. Possibly because she didn't have much confidence herself . . .

SOPHIE. What did she do?

FRANCOIS. And here we are!

ROBERT. When we were together she was finishing her post grad thesis and doing a bit of catwalk work to get by . . .

SOPHIE. She was a model!?

FRANCOIS *is making frantic signals at* ROBERT. *They're all talking at once, cutting in on each other.*

ROBERT. Yes . . . now and then . . . but she wasn't really interested in it . . .

SOPHIE. And she was finishing a post grad degree?

ROBERT. Eh . . . yes . . . but she was a total mess, you wouldn't believe it . . . and her sweat had this really strong smell . . .

SOPHIE. Was she anorexic?

ROBERT. . . . Really unpleasant . . .

FRANCOIS. Great coffee.

ROBERT. Anorexic? . . . Eh . . . no, I don't think so . . .

SOPHIE. Oh yes . . . it's very hard to recognise it in the early stages you know.

FRANCOIS. Sophie . . . eh Genevieve, did you know Robert was a runner? (*To* ROBERT.) Genevieve's a runner, loves it.

SOPHIE. Because they say models are anorexic. I saw a documentary about it.

FRANCOIS. Robert, tell us about the time you did the marathon twice in one day.

SOPHIE. Skeletons, that's what you want to turn us into.

ROBERT. Eh? I've never done the marathon twice in one day.

FRANCOIS. Tell us anyway.

SOPHIE. It's horrible. I've heard some of them have all sorts of things removed just to lose weight. Livers, ribs, intestines . . . then they get the whole lot shoved up into their breasts.

FRANCOIS. Genevieve!

SOPHIE. What is it?

FRANCOIS. You've no idea what you're talking about.

SOPHIE. Anyway they get bits of their stomachs cut out so they lose their appetites; when you think of all those Chinese people dying of hunger . . .

FRANCOIS. There's people in Québec dying of hunger.

SOPHIE. Eh? I know that.

ROBERT. Well you know beauty and charm are far more subtle than fashionable aesthetic criteria.

SOPHIE. You see François? Robert agrees with me. Models are ugly.

Scene Thirteen

Night. A change of music. We hear the sound of kisses, goodbyes, thank yous, see you soon, etc.

SOPHIE. What a great night!

FRANCOIS. Are you serious?

SOPHIE. Of course, why?

FRANCOIS. You never stopped taking chunks out of each other!

SOPHIE. No, I never stopped taking chunks out of him.

FRANCOIS. Oh yeah, you were off the leash. I wasn't too comfortable with that actually, that felt like you were settling scores with me, like some kind of transference thing.

SOPHIE. No. It was all him, he never stopped pushing me. I bet he was trying to discover my personality.

FRANCOIS. You're not usually as confrontational as that.

SOPHIE. Well if I don't really like a guy its easy to be all gentle and laid-back . . .

FRANCOIS. You like him?

SOPHIE. Yes!

FRANCOIS. I don't understand anything.

SOPHIE. Couldn't you tell?

FRANCOIS. Not really, no.

SOPHIE. Aw I've ruined everything. Oh he's going to think I'm a right idiot.

FRANCOIS. No . . .

SOPHIE. So why did he shoot off?

FRANCOIS. Because it's two in the morning!

SOPHIE. *No!*

FRANCOIS. Eh . . . yeah.

SOPHIE. I usually crash about eleven.

FRANCOIS. I know, you always flake out on me.

SOPHIE. Maybe this means he's the one.

FRANCOIS. Maybe . . .

SOPHIE. Right, I'm off, thanks for everything. I'm sorry to leave you with so much washing up but I'm whacked . . . Hey François?

FRANCOIS. What?

SOPHIE. If he liked me why didn't he offer to drive me home?

FRANCOIS. You brought your car!

SOPHIE. But he doesn't know that.

FRANCOIS. Well yeah, anyone can see you've got a car.

SOPHIE. Eh?

FRANCOIS. I don't know, you've just got the look of a car owner.

SOPHIE. How can you have the look of a car owner?

FRANCOIS. Whatever, he really liked you. I sensed it.

SOPHIE. You sensed it? I mean really?

FRANCOIS. Yeah, yeah.

SOPHIE. I thought so too.

FRANCOIS. There you go.

SOPHIE. You sensed something then?

FRANCOIS. Oh yeah, it was like a sign, an energy, an aura, all that. I felt all that.

SOPHIE. You're winding me up!

FRANCOIS. No, no.

SOPHIE. OK, I'm off. Oh François?

FRANCOIS. What?

SOPHIE. His ex isn't even called Sophie. He told me she wasn't called Sophie.

FRANCOIS. Eh . . . Oh that must have been another ex then. What I mean is not this last ex, an ex ex.

SOPHIE. Oh right. But if I'm going to see him again I don't want to be called Genevieve OK? You nearly got it wrong loads of times.

FRANCOIS. Yeah, yeah. I'll tell him. I'll explain.

SOPHIE. OK, good night then. Oh François?

FRANCOIS. What?

SOPHIE. When Robert said good night to me did you notice anything?

FRANCOIS. What?

SOPHIE. Well we did the kiss and he did sort of kiss me on the cheeks but actually he was quite close to my mouth . . . You know like . . . not really like you'd just kiss someone on the cheek . . . It was very subtle . . . I don't know if you noticed . . . No? . . . It was like he was ignoring that gap you're supposed to leave between the cheek and the mouth, see what I mean? . . . And he kind of kissed a bit harder a bit longer than you would if it was just a wee peck . . . didn't you notice that? Then he said 'Good to see you.' I think that's much more significant than 'See you.' Don't you think? Usually you say 'See you,' just like that, you know? I don't think you'd say 'Good to see you' unless you really meant it do you?

FRANCOIS. Sophie?

SOPHIE. What?

FRANCOIS. Good to see you.

SOPHIE. OK, goodnight.

Scene Fourteen

LEA. Dear Sophie,

François isn't scared of anything. He's not scared of ants, he's not scared of thunder, he's not scared of strangers, he's not scared of nightfall, he's not scared of all the giants that surround him. He still doesn't know how to walk, he doesn't know how to ask for directions, he doesn't know how to survive in the forest and yet he has no fear of life. How does he do it? I know how to walk, I know how to ask for directions and survive in the forest and I'm still scared of thunder, of nightfall, of all the giants who're bigger than me. And I'm scared of looking for you again and maybe finding you and you'll be a grown-up lady and I won't know you because you won't have your wee bunches. I'm still coming to Montreal, I'll drop in at that café with the man who inspired me to choose the name François. He looked just the way you described your husband, except he wasn't Italian.

I'll still send you this letter, just in case.

Your faithful Lea.

Scene Fifteen

At FRANCOIS*'s flat, a month later. Everyone is eating in silence, a little uncomfortable, polite smiles.*

FRANCOIS (*to audience*). For the next three weeks Robert didn't appear in the café to listen to François's stories and Sophie didn't call François to tell him her conquests.

FRANCOIS *looks at* ROBERT *and* SOPHIE. *He breaks the silence.*

Well I just can't believe you two got together.

SOPHIE. OK believe it François. You're repeating yourself.

FRANCOIS. No but don't you think it's weird? I have these two friends and now here's this couple. It's funny. It's really funny. And it's all my doing.

ROBERT. Have you got the right time Darling?

FRANCOIS. You're onto 'Darling' already?

SOPHIE. François!

FRANCOIS. After three weeks together you're calling her 'Darling'!?

ROBERT. Well . . .

FRANCOIS. It's just I always ask myself if the first time you call your girlfriend 'Darling' it's because you're sick of her name. Although Genevieve is pretty. It's worth thinking about the stages you go through with pet names in a relationship, it's a very intriguing phenomenon, don't you think?

ROBERT. So François, how are you doing?

FRANCOIS. Fantastic. Couldn't be better. I've decided to get serious about trying to find some funding for my film.

SOPHIE. Oh well done! About time.

FRANCOIS. That's right, when we were together you'd get really stressed out when I didn't work on my film, eh Genevieve? You see Robert she felt responsible for my dreams, isn't that lovely? You've got no chance of taking it easy. You'll see.

SOPHIE. You're being a bit weird tonight François.

FRANCOIS. Ach no, come on, I'll get the dessert.

FRANCOIS *exits.* ROBERT *and* SOPHIE *wait in silence, very uncomfortable.* FRANCOIS *is singing loudly in the kitchen.* ROBERT *takes* SOPHIE*'s hand. As* FRANCOIS *comes back she lets go again.*

Now isn't that sensitive? You won't hold hands while I'm here. Is that sensitivity or embarassment? I'd like to believe it's sensitivity to poor, single, lonely me. Taste the cake before I break down altogether.

ROBERT (*the cake*). Wow François! That looks amazing!

SOPHIE. Yes, look at you making desserts!

FRANCOIS. It wasn't me it was the caterer. All I did was chuck it on one of my plates to fool you. Shazzam.

Pause.

Have you just got the one library ticket or one each?

SOPHIE. What?

FRANCOIS. When you get books out the library, have you got one card for the two of you or have you got two cards?

ROBERT. Eh?

FRANCOIS. Because with my first proper girlfriend we registered together at the library on one card, in my name, and when we split up she took out all these books on my card and she never brought them back, it was a big problem . . .

ROBERT. You know, it's a funny thing but I think I might have a headache . . .

SOPHIE. You're not sleeping at the moment. We should go . . .

FRANCOIS. Take a paracetamol, you'll be fine. A wee coffee.

SOPHIE. I think we're going to make a move François, look at us, we're dropping here.

FRANCOIS. So take a paracetamol! Aw don't do this to me, you've still got to read my cards Genevieve.

ROBERT. No I've really got a headache . . .

SOPHIE. Another time François. OK?

FRANCOIS. I've known you ten years and the first time I actually do want you to read my cards you're off! The one time I do want to know my future, try and take some control of my life and you're both running out on me . . .

SOPHIE. François, give me a ring in the morning, OK?

FRANCOIS. Please Sophie. Don't go.

SOPHIE. François . . .

ROBERT. 'Sophie'?

FRANCOIS. Sophie do my cards! I need to know what's going to happen to me. Do my cards Sophie, when we were together you always wanted to and I always said it was a pile of crap . . .

ROBERT. Why is he calling you Sophie?

SOPHIE. I don't know! François stop it!

FRANCOIS. Well poor wee Robert, if only you'd read my crappy screenplay instead of pretending to give lectures you might actually have a clue.

ROBERT. Eh?

SOPHIE. What are you talking about? I don't understand a thing here!

ROBERT. You're Sophie?

SOPHIE. Yes my name's Sophie. What's the problem?

ROBERT. François is this *the* Sophie? I mean is this the woman who pushes doors instead of pulling them?

SOPHIE. What have you been saying about me François?

FRANCOIS. Well now we're even Robert because you've been telling me a few porkies too haven't you? You don't teach at the university.

SOPHIE. What?

ROBERT. What do you mean? Of course I teach . . .

FRANCOIS. I tried to leave a message for you at the university calling off this dinner, because I just had a feeling it was going to turn nasty. They told me you got the boot two years ago.

SOPHIE. Eh? What's the story here?

Lighting change, flashback. ROBERT *is addressing imaginary students.*

ROBERT. The carelessness with which you've had the audacity to undertake your studies forces me to consider several possible conclusions. Earlier I asked your opinion of a required text. Two possiblities. There are those amongst you who have offered me their opinion of a work they have manifestly failed to read, disgusting sloth, or, which they have failed to understand, determined imbecility, worse than sloth. But a further and worse possibility, most prevalent this year, is that there are those who have read the book in question but yet have no idea what the phrase 'to give one's opinion' actually means. You have no opinions, no vision, no personalities. It's sad. You think you're giving me your opinion and you're actually regurgitating a plot synopsis. I have read *A la recherche du temps perdu* and I need neither a summary or a vulgarisation of that work. Do you seriously believe that if you write 'I think' at the start of each sentence you're giving me your insights? Your opinions? I've met Fresian cows who had greater intellectual capacity. If I realised I was like you, with no understanding of my head or my heart, I'd be ashamed to go on living. You're a waste of paper, of ink and of air. I'm going to tell you something: you are useless little shits. And you think you're so clever because you made it into university do you?

SOPHIE. OK, so he did lay it on a bit strong . . .

FRANCOIS. No, no, this is good . . .

ROBERT. Well answer me! You think you're intelligent, set up for life, your toe poised on the first step of the ladder? You're always talking about your rights, grabbing any excuse to set up another committee . . . Do you realise that the privilege of attending university comes with responsibilities too, including the responsibility of not boring me to death with your continual banalities! Boredom is dangerous. It creates people like you. But then I realise that the administration of this institution, corrupted as it is by money, is devoid of any moral scruples and happy to be so.

FRANCOIS. Oh no, not the administration.

ROBERT. Because they offer a useless syllabus. Literature. Come on. That's for people so ovine, so satiated with their own stupidity that they never open a book unless they have an essay due on it next month. I therefore permit myself to vomit upon this institution, on its complacency, on your sloth and upon you.

Return to present.

SOPHIE. You said that?

ROBERT. They forced me to take a sabbatical afterwards, claiming that I must be exhausted. There was a petition to support me.

With one name on it. The ugly girl's. If she'd been good-looking I'd've definitely fallen in love with her.

SOPHIE. So then what?

ROBERT. I signed on for a while, I hitched my way around Québec and now I . . . well I get by.

SOPHIE. And how long were you going to hide all this from me? How many times would I have picked you up from the university thinking how good you looked on the stairs there with your books and your little glasses . . . ?

FRANCOIS. You pick him up from the university?

ROBERT. I was going to tell you . . . I was going to tell you both . . .

FRANCOIS. She never picked me up from the university . . . Sophie did you ever pick me up from the university when I was at university?

SOPHIE. I can't believe you've lied to me like this. Essays lying out on your desk waiting to be marked, all those lesson plans you had to get ready for the morning, all your little set-ups, just who exactly were you trying to kid?

ROBERT. Would you have wanted to meet an unemployed man called Robert? 'Sophie, I'd like you to meet a really great guy, he's called Robert . . . What? . . . Oh he's really interesting. He's on the dole.' See what I mean Sophie! Everyone dropped me instantly because these days we're only defined by what we do for a living. Tell me your profession and I'll tell you what you're worth.

LEA *enters.*

LEA (*to audience*). But it wouldn't bother me what he did with his time, as long as we spent it together.

ROBERT (*to* SOPHIE). It'd bother you, because the whole world would make sure it did, 'And what does your husband do? Nothing? You mean nothing at all? Nothing but love you? You poor thing . . . '

LEA. That's enough for me.

SOPHIE. OK it's true. It would bother me, I wouldn't be able stop it.

ROBERT. . . . No job, no ambition, a man who just spends his days reading and travelling . . .

LEA. I think that's real ambition: to want to read and see beautiful things . . .

SOPHIE (*to* LEA). Yeah but you always had your head in the clouds.

LEA. I love him that's all.

LEA *exits,* FRANCOIS *is lost in thought,* SOPHIE *and* ROBERT *are watching him.*

SOPHIE. Well?

FRANCOIS. Sorry? What?

SOPHIE. Explain yourself! Tell us why you wanted me to call myself Genevieve when Robert here just told me he never had an ex called Sophie.

FRANCOIS. What?

SOPHIE. Why is everyone lying here? What is your problem? Why did you tell me Robert worked at the university if it wasn't true? Did Robert know that you knew he'd got the boot? Why are you both toying with me like this? What is it you want François? Oh, is that your real name? François?

FRANCOIS. What I want to know is this; would it have changed anything if I'd run after you in the rain?

SOPHIE. What?

FRANCOIS. Because it wasn't my fault it wasn't raining that day.

SOPHIE. What are you talking about?

FRANCOIS. Running in the sunshine, doesn't sound so meaningful somehow . . .

ROBERT. He's talking about when he called off the wedding.

SOPHIE. Eh?

ROBERT. It's OK. He told me all about it.

SOPHIE. But I was the one who called off the wedding.

Lighting change. Flashback.

FRANCOIS. God you wouldn't believe the number of friends I've got. The whole world wants to be my friend. All the women I know want me to be their friend, their brother, their big cuddly teddy bear. Talk about lucky, I'm swimming in female friendship.

SOPHIE. No stop it François, tell me you don't hate me, tell me we can still be friends.

FRANCOIS. I've got dozens of wonderful friends. Why would I need your friendship?

SOPHIE. I know you're disappointed François . . .

FRANCOIS. Disappointed? I'm disappointed when I miss the previews at the cinema. Don't talk to me about disappointed.

SOPHIE. Bastard door!

FRANCOIS. Oh spare me the door routine!

ROBERT. You have to pull it . . .

SOPHIE. I know you have to pull it! I want him to ask me to stay!

ROBERT. She wants you to ask her to stay.

FRANCOIS. Stay Sophie. I don't hate you. We can still be friends.

Return to present.

FRANCOIS (*to audience*). Then we spent the rest of the night getting totally off our faces.

Time lapse during which the characters are understood to have been drinking. They're all a bit drunk and happy.

SOPHIE. You don't hate me eh Robert? We can still be friends?

ROBERT. God aye. You've got to be less trouble as a friend.

FRANCOIS. Don't you believe it.

SOPHIE. Oy! Shut it you! So where's this wine got to?

FRANCOIS. We've drunk it all. I've only got whisky left.

ROBERT. Ah, whisky . . .

FRANCOIS. Thought you had a headache?

ROBERT. A wee paracetamol and a whisky please, neat.

SOPHIE. Robert, I don't want you thinking we're splitting up because you don't teach at the university. That's not the reason . . .

SOPHIE *and* ROBERT (*together*). It's just that I/you don't know which way is up right now and I/you need some time alone.

ROBERT. You explained all that. I don't hate you. We'll still be friends.

SOPHIE. Come on guys, I'll read your cards, OK?

FRANCOIS. Oh no, not that.

SOPHIE. OK so I'll do my own cards. See I want to know if I'll get married and have kids one day. And who with. And then I'll go and find that guy and grab him by the ears and say 'What time do you call this!?'

FRANCOIS. Poor guy, he hasn't even got here and he's already in trouble.

ROBERT. Hey Sophie . . .

SOPHIE. What?

ROBERT. Do my cards.

FRANCOIS. Robert, don't believe any of it, she makes it all up.

SOPHIE. François will you just stop it . . .

FRANCOIS. Aye but you told me you just pretended and you hadn't a scooby how to read cards, and you just ended up telling people what they want to hear.

SOPHIE. Well I make people happy that way.

ROBERT. That's very good. Very noble. Come on Sophie tell me what I want to hear. Let's see if you're any good.

SOPHIE *lays out the cards.*

Come on. Tell me what I want to hear.

SOPHIE. Oh I can see so many things in this Robert. You're going to be part of an extraordinary story. Something even François couldn't make up. It's wild. I've never seen such beautiful cards. You are going to be part of a story that's so totally over the top you couldn't even put it in a film.

Scene Sixteen

FRANCOIS*'s café.*

FRANCOIS (*to audience*). It would be a story of strange rediscoveries, of people suddenly bursting into each other's lives, a story of little things that can turn the whole world inside out.

LEA *enters.*

We're closed.

LEA. Again? If you're closed you could lock the door.

FRANCOIS. Hey I remember you.

LEA. Hullo François.

FRANCOIS. You remember my name?

LEA. Yes.

FRANCOIS. Are you still travelling around?

LEA. No. I've moved to Montreal.

FRANCOIS. Oh aye?

LEA. Yes. I've sold my bed and breakfast, now I'm opening another in the middle of town.

FRANCOIS. Oh aye?

LEA. I'm so excited. Montreal stinks. It's brilliant.

FRANCOIS. Eh?

LEA. What I mean is there's people everywhere, cars, pollution . . . it's so alive.

FRANCOIS. Well yeah you're right there . . . Did you have a boy or a girl?

LEA. A boy. François. My mother's looking after him while I get myself settled.

FRANCOIS. So . . . did you find your friend Sophie in the end?

LEA. No, to be honest I wonder if I'd even recognise her on the street without her two wee bunches.

SOPHIE *enters.*

SOPHIE. Lea?

LEA. Sophie!

FRANCOIS. You two know each other?

LEA *and* SOPHIE. Yes.

LEA. Did you get my letters?

SOPHIE. No.

LEA. No, I didn't get your letters either.

SOPHIE. . . .

LEA. You didn't write me any letters?

SOPHIE. No.

LEA. Not even a wee one that you forgot to post and you were actually going to post tomorrow and it's in your bag?

SOPHIE. No.

LEA. It's because you were worried I'd find all the spelling mistakes like I did when we were little isn't it?

SOPHIE. Yes.

LEA. Did you really call your daughter Lea?

SOPHIE. No.

LEA. What did you call her?

SOPHIE. I don't have a daughter. No kids. No husband. No new house.

LEA. And you haven't stopped biting your nails either?

SOPHIE. No.

LEA. You were playing at happy, contented grown-up ladies?

SOPHIE. That's it.

LEA. I wish you'd told me we were playing. I could have joined in.

SOPHIE. Oh Lea, I'm so sorry.

LEA. I'd like to play happy, contented grown-up ladies with you again Sophie. Do you remember those unbelievable hats and the high-heeled shoes that gave us vertigo, and we had tea and we talked about our maids and our jewels and our horses and our husbands and it was all just made up for the game but that didn't matter because we were making it up together. And then you went on playing without telling me but you're not even wearing an unbelievable hat and I'm betting high heels stopped giving you vertigo years ago, so what's the point of still playing at grown-up ladies?

SOPHIE. I was going to write and tell you the truth soon. I was going to write when I was happy.

FRANCOIS. Do you girls want something to drink?

LEA. And what if that never happened?

SOPHIE. That's right! Tell me I'll never be happy!

FRANCOIS. . . . a wee coffee with a shot in it? Anything?

SOPHIE. François, you've no idea of what's appropriate to the moment have you?

LEA. You two know each other?

FRANCOIS *and* SOPHIE. Yes.

FRANCOIS (*to* SOPHIE). You told me that was absolutely what you loved about me.

SOPHIE. What?

FRANCOIS. You did. You said that.

SOPHIE. You're right. OK. I said that.

FRANCOIS. You told me that I had no idea of what's appropriate, no taste, but that you loved me for all the things I didn't have, that I was the most original person you'd ever met. You told me that I was like a surprise that never stopped surprising you and . . .

ROBERT *enters.*

ROBERT. Hi.

FRANCOIS. I was just thinking there was someone missing.

FRANCOIS *and* SOPHIE. Hi Robert.

LEA. Hi Robert.

ROBERT. Lea!

FRANCOIS *and* SOPHIE. You two know each other?

LEA *and* ROBERT. Yes.

A long pause.

LEA. Well what can you say at a moment like this?

ROBERT. You look well.

LEA. It's the city air.

ROBERT. I missed you.

LEA. Really?

FRANCOIS *and* SOPHIE *talk to each other at the same time as* ROBERT *and* LEA, *overlapping dialogue.*

FRANCOIS. And you also said you loved the way I looked when I thought no one was watching me.

ROBERT. Lea, I've dreamed of meeting you like this . . .

SOPHIE. You're right. I did say that. Here, have a strawberry.

ROBERT. You'd tell me you'd been searching frantically for me, to tell me we'd made a baby together in the wet grass . . .

FRANCOIS. You bought strawberries?

SOPHIE. I stopped by the market.

LEA. And I'd tell you he's called François.

ROBERT. And I'd tell you that's perfect.

FRANCOIS. But they're not in season.

SOPHIE. No but it's better when they're not in season.

LEA. But you told me you wanted to love with no thought for tomorrow.

ROBERT. Yes but then it was tomorrow and I wanted it again.

FRANCOIS. You told me you liked the way I said goodbye, as if I was asking a question.

LEA. And you told me you didn't want Christmas pudding and family and all that traditional stuff.

ROBERT. We could have a trifle instead.

SOPHIE. And I told you I didn't ever want to risk losing you, today or any other day.

FRANCOIS. You didn't say that. You said you didn't know if I was responsible enough to start a family.

SOPHIE. Yes but what I wanted to say was that I didn't ever want to risk losing you, that day or any other day.

ROBERT. Why didn't you call me?

LEA. I was scared you'd given me a fake number.

SOPHIE. What I wanted to say was . . .

LEA. Anyway you told me you wanted to love with no thought for tomorrow!

SOPHIE. They're good strawberries eh?

ROBERT. I forgot to tell you that I wanted to stay with you till tomorrow and that tomorrow I'd want the same thing and the day after and the one after that until your hair was white.

FRANCOIS. They're the best strawberries I've ever eaten.

LEA. And when my hair was white?

ROBERT. We'd go on honeymoon again.

LEA. On honeymoon?

SOPHIE. One day I nearly told you none of them were anything next to you. None of the Italians, none of the others, not even the ones in films. The ones in films are nothing at all if you take away the music.

ROBERT. And we'd get ourselves thrown out of every hotel and every bed and breakfast because we'd make so much noise being happy.

LEA. Yes.

SOPHIE. I nearly told you all that, I tried it out in front of the mirror and I was really ridiculous so I never said anything.

LEA. But don't you think this is a bit sudden?

SOPHIE. I would have told you that we should get married, we should get married in winter because everything tastes better when it isn't in season. And you would have said . . .

ROBERT. You know everyone gets married with no idea what they're doing. Let's have no idea what we're doing. Let's get married and work it out later. Like everyone else.

FRANCOIS. Yes.

LEA. Yes.

Scene Seventeen

An extravagant tableau of a double wedding under the January snow. FRANCOIS and SOPHIE, ROBERT and LEA. The music is Mozart's Coronation Mass. The four characters walk forward and pose, frozen, in the lights of flashing cameras.

FRANCOIS. An extravagant tableau of a double wedding under the January snow. François and Sophie, Robert and Lea. The music is Mozart's Coronation Mass. The four characters walk forward and pose, frozen, in the lights of flashing cameras.

Fade to black.